THE SWORD OF GOLIATH

Isaiah 54,17

TOMMY COMBS

+ Combs

THE SWORD OF GOLIATH
© Copyright 2007
by Tommy Combs

All Scripture is taken from
the Holy Bible, King James Version.

ISBN: 0-9774223-9-9

Published by

LifeBridge
BOOKS
P.O. BOX 49428
CHARLOTTE, NC 28277

Printed in the United States of America.

DEDICATION

To my precious wife, Linda—
the best gift God ever gave me.
To my son, Matthew—a Prince with God.
To my daughter, Sara Elizabeth
—God's Princess.

CONTENTS

INTRODUCTION

As a boy, I loved to hear the story of how a young shepherd named David challenged the mighty warrior, Goliath. Armed only with a simple slingshot, he defeated the feared giant.

When I grew older and began to study God's Word, the story took on even greater meaning. David not only conquered the enemy, he marched up to Goliath, unsheathed the Philistines's sword and used it to finish the job!

One of the most powerful verses in Scripture declares: *"No weapon that is formed against thee shall prosper"* (Isaiah 54:17). This means what the enemy plans for your destruction can become the answer for your deliverance.

You will discover this divine principle in the lives of Daniel, Esther, Joseph, the three Hebrew children, and Jesus Himself.

On these pages you will learn how to turn the

tables on trouble and claim total victory.

Most important, I want to share how you can apply this great lesson to your own circumstances to conquer the forces that come against you and build a wall of protection around those you love.

I pray the words of this book will build your faith and give you spiritual authority as you fulfill God's vision for your future.

– Tommy Combs

CHAPTER ONE

THE STONE AND THE SWORD

*So David prevailed over the Philistine
with a sling and with a stone, and smote the
Philistine, and slew him; but there was no sword
in the hand of David. Therefore David ran, and stood
upon the Philistine, and took his sword, and drew it
out of the sheath thereof, and slew him, and cut
off his head therewith. And when the Philistines
saw their champion was dead, they fled.*

– I SAMUEL 17:50-51

In Israel's valley of Elah, about 15 miles southwest of Bethlehem, one of the classic conflicts of all time took place. It happened during the 11th century BC.

Every child in Sunday school can tell you the story of a teenage shepherd named David who came up against the giant, Goliath, but the significance of how the conflict ended contains a powerful message for you and me.

On one hill were amassed the armies of King Saul, and on the other hill were the forces of the Philistines.

Both sides came ready for battle, yet there was absolutely nothing going on. Day after day, the enemies just looked across the valley at each other.

At this point in time the Philistines were far more powerful than the Israelites—and had even captured the Ark of the Covenant.

"GIVE ME A MAN"

In this tense standoff, one Philistine warrior stepped out from his troops, stood in the middle of the Elah valley and, with a loud, booming voice, called out to the Israelite army: *"Why are ye come out to set your battle in array? am not I a*

Philistine, and ye servants to Saul? choose you a man for you, and let him come down to me. If he be able to fight with me, and to kill me, then will we be your servants: but if I prevail against him, and kill him, then shall ye be our servants, and serve us. And the Philistine said, I defy the armies of Israel this day; give me a man, that we may fight together" (vv.8-10).

The challenge was issued by a man from Gath named Goliath, whom the Bible says was *"six cubits and a span"* (1 Samuel 17:4)—that's nearly 10 feet tall! On his head was a bronze helmet and he was dressed in 126 pounds of armor. The tip of his spear alone weighed over fifteen pounds (vv.5-7).

When Saul and his army saw this giant and heard his words, they were terrified!

When Saul and his army saw this giant and heard his words, they were terrified!

A DISRUPTIVE FORCE

Every morning and evening Goliath issued the

same challenge. It was a deliberate act to provoke and unnerve the Israelites. In these days, it was the custom for Jews to pray a prayer called the "Shema" twice a day. They were following the command of (Deuteronomy 6:8) and in remembrance of the sacrifice offered each morning and evening by the children of Israel (Numbers 28:4).

Guess who shows up at prayer time?

They prayed, "Hear, O Israel. The Lord God is one God and no enemy shall stand before thee."

Guess who shows up at prayer time? Goliath.

Now, thousands of years later, our enemy is still Satan and he is using the same old tactics—attempting to disrupt us every time we call on God. The devil will do everything in his power to ruin your day and make you his slave.

Back in the valley of Elah, the giant stepped forward to repeat his challenge and torment Saul's armies every morning and evening for 40 long days.

The number 40 is important in scripture:

- It rained for 40 days in the time of Noah's flood (Genesis 7:4).
- The children of Israel wandered in the desert for 40 years (Numbers 32:13).
- Jesus was in the wilderness for 40 days (Luke 4:2).
- The Son of God fasted 40 days and 40 nights (Matthew 4:2).

Forty represents a time of testing, but think of the rejoicing and victory which comes on day 41!

WHERE WAS THE ARMOR?

Since King Saul was the General in charge of the Israeli army, he should have been the one who stepped up the plate to fight Goliath, yet he didn't dare? Why? Because Saul had disobeyed the Almighty and the power of God's anointing had left him. The Bible tells us, *"...the the spirit of the Lord departed from Saul"* (1 Samuel 16:14).

The battle gear he should have been wearing was in the tent with the armor bearer. Essentially, the army of Israel had no leader!

A SPECIAL ANOINTING

Here is where young David, the son of Jesse, enters the picture.

The three oldest sons in the family, Eliab, Abinadab and Shammah were fighting in Saul's army, but the youngest of Jesse's eight boys, David, was tending his father's sheep back in Bethlehem.

Remember, unbeknown to Saul and on direct orders from God, David had been anointed by the high priest Samuel to be the next king of Israel (1 Samuel 16:13), yet no one considered him as a warrior to fight against the Philistines.

One day, curious to know what was happening on the battlefield, Jesse told David, "Take this sack of food to your brothers in the camp, and give these wedges of cheese to the captain of their division." He said, *"...look how thy brethren fare"* (1 Samuel 17:8).

"WHAT'S GOING ON?"

Early the next morning, David was on his way to the camp. Just as he arrived the army was moving into battle formation, shouting their war cry.

David left the parcels of food in care of a sentry, and quickly ran out to the troops to greet his three brothers. It was about that time Goliath stepped out to give his usual challenge—and the shepherd boy heard it with his own ears. He asked, "What is going on here?"

The minute the Israelites saw the giant, they once

> *"What is going*
> *on here?"*

more cowered and retreated in fear. They said, *"Have ye seen this man that is come up? surely to defy Israel is he come up: and it shall be, that the man who killeth him, the king will enrich him with great riches, and will give him his daughter, and make his father's house free in Israel"* (v.25).

This sounded rather intriguing to David—a huge reward, one of Saul's daughters as a bride and no more taxes for the family!

"WHY AREN'T YOU BACK HOME?"

David asked the soldiers standing around him, *"...who is this uncircumcised Philistine, that he should defy the armies of the living God?"* (v.26).

The word "uncircumcised" was a code word for someone who had no relationship with the living God—a man who relied on idols.

Eliab, David's older brother, heard him talking to the troops and became quite angry. "What in the world are you doing here? Why aren't you back home minding your own business and taking care of the sheep? He added, *"I know thy pride, and the naughtiness of thine heart; for thou art come down that thou mightest see the battle"* (v.28).

David ignored his brother and talked again about how this Philistine must be killed. A messenger rushed to Saul to report what David was saying, and Saul sent for him.

LIONS AND BEARS

When they meet, David confidently told the king, *"Let no man' heart fail because of him; thy servant will go and fight with this Philistine"* (v.32).

Saul could hardly believe his ears and warned David, *"Thou art not able to go against this Philistine to fight with him: for thou art but a youth, and he a man of war from his youth"* (v.33).

Trying to assure him, David said, "Look, when I've been tending sheep for my father and a lion or a bear took a lamb from the flock, I charged in and rescued the lamb. And if it came after me, I'd grab its throat, break its neck and kill it!" Then he added, "I'll do the same thing to this Philistine!"

"I'd grab its throat, break its neck and kill it!"

How could this young man have enough confidence to boldly say such a thing? Because he was anointed of God and believed Jehovah would protect him and deliver Goliath into his hands.

Saul was ready to take a chance. Immediately,

he *"... armed David with his armour, and he put an helmet of brass upon his head"* (v.38).

FORGET THE ARMOR!

I believe the reason Saul wanted to cover David in his full battle gear and send him down the mountain to fight the giant was to fool his own soldiers into thinking it was the king himself who had finally accepted the challenge of this taunting enemy.

> *David had only one objective—to please God.*

Saul was only interested in pleasing the people and preserving his image. David, however, had only one objective—to please God.

When the heavy armor was draped around David, he said, "I can't fight with all this on me. I'm not used to it." So, *"...David put them off him"* (v.39).

Instead, he took his shepherd's staff, went down to the brook, chose five smooth stones and carefully put them in his pack. And, armed only with his sling in his hand, he walked straight toward Goliath in the middle of the valley.

In his heart, David knew this was not a human confrontation between he and the giant. It was spiritual warfare and only faith in God would bring triumph.

THE GIANT LAUGHED

Here was the Philistine, pacing back and forth with his shield bearer in front of him. When the giant saw this young boy approaching he was amused and began to openly laugh and mock him.

The Bible says, *"...he disdained him: for he was but a youth, and ruddy, and of a fair countenance. And the Philistine said unto David, Am I a dog, that thou comest to me with staves? And the Philistine cursed David by his gods"* (vv.42-43). And he added, *"Come to me, and I will give thy flesh unto the fowls of the air, and to the beasts of the field"* (v.44).

These harsh words didn't bother David in the least. He shouted back to Goliath, *"Thou comest to me with a sword, and with a spear, and with a shield: but I come to thee in the name of the Lord of hosts, the God of the armies of Israel, whom thou hast defied. This day will the Lord deliver thee into mine hand; and I will smite thee, and take thine head from thee; and I will give the carcases of the host of the Philistines this day unto the fowls of the air, and to the wild beasts of the earth; that all the earth may know that there is a God in Israel. And all this assembly shall know that the LORD saveth not with sword and spear: for the battle is the Lord's, and he will give you into our hands"* (vv.45-47).

DEFYING ALL ODDS

The now-aroused giant started toward the shepherd boy—and unflinching, David started running straight for Goliath. He then reached into his bag and took one of his five stones, put it into his sling and hurled it a the giant.

Scripture tells us he *"...smote the Philistine in his forehead, that the stone sunk into his forehead; and he fell upon his face to the earth"* (v.49).

Defying all odds—with no sword or spear in his hand—David achieved what the entire Israeli army was unable to

David achieved what the entire Israeli army was unable to accomplish.

accomplish. In an instant, the most feared warrior in the land was face down in the valley of Elah.

KILLED BY HIS OWN SWORD!

To finish the job, David ran forward, stood over him and pulled the giant's sword from its sheath. Then with a final act of victory, he brought the sharp blade down and cut off the head of Goliath (v.51).

When the Philistine army realized their champion was dead, they started running for their lives.

Across the valley, however, a huge celebration was under way. Scripture records, *"And the men* of Israel and of Judah arose, and shouted, and pursued the Philistines, until thou come to the valley, and to the gates of Ekron. And the wounded of the Philistines fell down by the way to Shaaraim, even unto Gath, and unto Ekron" (v.52).

The word quickly spread, and when the battle was won, "...the women came out of all cities of Israel, singing and dancing, to meet king Saul, with tabrets, with joy, and with instruments of music. And the women answered one another as they played, and said, Saul hath slain his thousands, and David his ten thousands" (1 Samuel 18:6-7).

Saul had no choice but to elevate David to a place of leadership in Israel.

CONFOUNDING THE WISE

Think of the significance of this victory. David cut Goliath's head off with his own sword. That is just like God. He will give you the power to take what the enemy tries to use against you and turn it around for your good—and His glory!

- Age doesn't matter—you can be seven, seventeen or seventy and the Lord will use you to destroy the enemy.
- Color doesn't matter—God is no respecter of persons (Acts 10:34).
- Experience doesn't matter—even if it is your first conflict, with the Lord on your side you will be victorious.

Always remember: *"God hath chosen the foolish things of the world to confound the wise; and God hath chosen the weak things of the world to confound the things which are mighty"* (1 Corinthians 1:27).

THE BATTLE IS THE LORD'S

The Almighty isn't concerned over your physical sword, shield or helmet. He will equip you for battle with the "whole armor of God" to combat the enemy. *"Stand therefore, having your loins girt about with truth, and having on the breastplate of righteousness; And your feet shod with the preparation of the gospel of peace; Above all, taking the shield of faith, wherewith ye shall be able to quench all the fiery darts of the wicked. And take the helmet of salvation, and the sword of the Spirit, which is the word of God"* (Ephesians 6:14-17).

With confidence you can come against the Goliaths of this world in the name of Jehovah—the Lord of Hosts. And even if your foe has a weapon, God will allow you to use it against him.

Even if your foe has a weapon, God will allow you to use it against him.

Remember, as David declared, *"...the battle is the Lord's"* (1 Samuel 17:47). With the Almighty by your side you are more than a conqueror and He will give the enemy into your hands.

NOT BY MIGHT OR POWER

The source of David's strength was given to

him long before this encounter. Scripture tells us that at the time of his anointing by Samuel, *"...from that day on the Spirit of the Lord came upon David in power"* (1 Samuel 16:13).

My friend, this exact same anointing is available to you. As David later wrote, *"Our help is in the name of the Lord, the Maker of heaven and earth"* (Psalm 124:8). Truly it is *"Not by might, nor by power, but by my spirit, saith the Lord of hosts"* (Zechariah 46).

The Almighty is the one who brings triumph. He alone delivers—not with our own sword or spear. Victory is ours when we are filled with His Word and led by His Spirit.

This very day, run toward your Giant and the Lord will be by your side. Let God be God!

What the Father did for David, He will do for you!

CHAPTER TWO

THE ULTIMATE DECISION

Then these men assembled, and found Daniel praying and making supplication before his God.
— DANIEL 6:11

Life is a constant series of decisions. Every day we chose what we will eat, how we will dress and who we will call on our cell phone. There are big choices too—the career we will embark on, who we will marry and the home we will buy. And the decisions we make concerning our children can affect their lives forever.

Yet, there is one choice which I call "The Ultimate Decision"—which determines life or death, heaven or hell. You decide the answer when you ask this question: Will I serve God or not?

Will I serve God or not?

This is the story of a young man who made the right choice.

"PERFECT SPECIMENS"

In the first chapter of Daniel we find Jerusalem being conquered by King Nebuchadnezzar of Babylon. One of his first acts was to instruct the head of his palace staff to find a few outstanding young Israelites and bring them to Babylon (modern day Iraq) where they would be taught the language of the Chaldeans.

The king was looking for young men, *"...in whom was no blemish, but well favoured, and skilful in all wisdom, and cunning in knowledge, and understanding science, and such as had ability in them to stand in the king' palace"* (Daniel 1:4).

These "perfect specimens" would be given a special diet from the royal table and after three years of training would be awarded prize assignments in the king's court.

Four of those chosen included Daniel, Hananiah, Mishael and Aszariah. (The last three we know by their new Babylonian names of Shadrach, Mechach and Abednego).

DANIEL MADE A DEAL

Early in his captivity, Daniel *"...purposed in his heart that he would not defile himself with the portion of the king's meat, nor with the wine which he drank"* (v.8). This decision set the tone for Daniel's life.

The head of the palace staff truly liked Daniel, but warned him, "Look, I'm responsible for your good health—and I'm afraid of what will happen if the king sees you are not as healthy as the rest. He'd have my head!"

Daniel made a deal. He convinced the steward to give him—and Shadrach, Meshach and Abednego—only vegetables and water for ten days, *"Then let our countenances be looked upon before thee, and the countenance of the children that eat of the portion of the king's meat: and as thou seest, deal with thy servants"* (v.13).

At the end of the test, Daniel was proven right; the four Israelites *did* look more robust than the others. So their exemption from the royal menu continued.

The Almighty gave these four young Israelites incredible wisdom and knowledge—the king found them *"...ten times better than all the magicians and astrologers that were in all his realm"* (v.20).

Daniel was especially gifted in the understanding of visions and dreams (v.17).

WHAT DOES IT MEAN?

During the second year of Nebuchadnezzar's reign, he had a dream none of his sorcerers or fortunetellers could interpret, but Daniel was used by God to explain the precise meaning to the king.

By doing this, the king made him a governor in Babylon. He was given favor in this heathen land because God showed him how to make the right decisions.

If you think everyone will be pleased when the Lord promotes you—think again! Those who refuse to fast and pray become extremely jealous when blessings and favor are poured out over those who do.

If you think everyone will be pleased when the Lord promotes you—think again!

The other princes in Babylon grew increasingly envious of Daniel's rise to power and looked for any excuse to find fault with him. Yet he continued to ascend in leadership through the reigns of Nebuchadnezzar and his son, King Belshazzar.

One night at the palace, the new king put on a feast for one thousand nobles, princes, wives and concubines. They were drinking wine from the gold and silver chalices his father had plundered from the Temple at Jerusalem—and in a drunken stupor they praised their idols and gods of brass and stone (Daniel 5:1-4).

WRITING ON THE WALL

Suddenly, out of nowhere, the fingers of a human hand appeared and began writing on the plaster of the palace wall—there was no physical body, just a hand.

> *Suddenly, out of nowhere, the fingers of a human hand appeared.*

Belshazzar was frightened beyond words. Scripture records, *"...the king's countenance was changed, and his thoughts troubled him, so that the joints of his loins were loosed, and his knees smote one against another"* (Daniel 5:6).

Urgently, he called for the soothsayers and astrologers of the land and promised that anyone who could read the writing on the wall would be *"...clothed with scarlet, and have a chain of gold about his neck, and shall be the third ruler in the kingdom"* (v.7).

"FOUND WANTING"

One seer after another attempted to determine the meaning, but failed. Then the king's wife remembered how Daniel had interpreted her father-in-laws dreams and he was immediately summoned. She described him as *"in whom is the spirit of the holy gods"* (v.11)

The Lord allowed Daniel to read the writing on the wall—yet the king didn't like what he heard one bit.

Daniel said: *"...this is the writing that was written, MENE, MENE, TEKEL, UPHARSIN. This is the interpretation of the thing: MENE; God hath numbered thy kingdom, and finished it. TEKEL; Thou art weighed in the balances, and art found wanting. PERES [UPHARSIN]; Thy kingdom is divided, and given to the Medes and Persians"* (vv.25-28).

However, true to his promise, the king clothed Daniel in scarlet, placed a gold chain around his neck and proclaimed him in charge of a third of the kingdom.

What happened next? The Bible says, *"In that night was Belshazzar the king of the Chaldeans slain"* (v.30).

THE KING'S DECREE

The next ruler of Babylon came to the throne—King Darius—and not only was Daniel one of the three leaders of the nation, but he *"...was preferred above the presidents and princes, because an excellent spirit was in him; and the king thought to set him over the whole realm"* (Daniel 6:3).

Darius grew to love Daniel—who was now in his 80s. He had proven to be a man of integrity, loyalty and honor who could be totally trusted.

This really annoyed the princes and they were determined to find a chink in his armor—something to end his rise to power.

Finally they said to one another, "The only fault we will ever find in him will be concerning the law of his God."

These jealous men knew that three times every day, with his windows opened toward the city of Jerusalem, Daniel would kneel and pray to his God, Jehovah.

So the princes, counselors and captains of the kingdom conspired together, wrote a decree, brought it to the royal palace and asked the king to sign it. The statute said: *"...whosoever shall ask a petition of any God or man for thirty days, save of thee, O king, he shall be cast into the den of lions"* (v.7).

As part of the administration of justice, any person who could survive a night with the lions would be declared innocent of the charges.

Darius put his signature on the dotted line.

Flattered, and not knowing the consequences, Darius put his signature on the dotted line. Then they reminded the king this was a law of the Medes and Persians, which could not be changed for any reason.

NO WAY OUT!

What did Daniel do when he learned of this new edict? He made the ultimate decision. He went home, opened his window, and prayed to the

Lord three times a day as usual (v.10). It was not to flagrantly challenge the decree, rather to continue worshiping God has he had always done. Nothing was going to change his mind or alter his actions concerning his commitment to the Lord.

God says, *"...them that honour me I will honour"* (1 Samuel 2:30).

------▶

Nothing was going to change his mind or alter his actions concerning his commitment to the Lord.

When the conspirators found him praying, they marched straight to the palace to remind Darius of the law he had approved.

"Hast thou not signed a decree, that every man that shall ask a petition of any God or man within thirty days, save of thee, O king, shall be cast into the den of lions? The king answered and said, The thing is true, according to the law of the Medes and Persians, which altereth not" (v.12).

They were more than happy to tell the king, "Daniel, one of the Jewish exiles, defies you. He is praying to his God three times a day."

Darius was upset with himself and tried to find a way to exempt Daniel from punishment. There was no way out—especially since Daniel proudly proclaimed his prayer life and wasn't about to deny it or change.

Daniel was brought before a disheartened Darius and sentenced to the den of lions.

THE DEN WAS SEALED

The lion is the king of the jungle—the most cunning of all animals. He may not be as large as an elephant, as fast as a chetah, as strong as a rhinoceros or as tall as a giraffe, but when a lion roars, all other creatures stop and take notice. And you certainly don't want to become dinner for a pack of hungry lions!

As the king commanded, Daniel was brought to the lion's den. But before he was thrown in, Darius spoke these revealing words: *"Thy God whom thou servest continually, he will deliver thee"* (v.16).

A large stone slab was placed over the mouth of

the den and the king sealed it with his own signet ring and the signet rings of all of his lords. It was final!

Hoping Against Hope

Darius spent a restless night, worried over Daniel's fate. And the next day, *"...the king arose very early in the morning, and went in haste unto the den of lions. And when he came to the den, he cried with a lamentable voice unto Daniel: and the king spake and said to Daniel, O Daniel, servant of the living God, is thy God, whom thou servest continually, able to deliver thee from the lions?"* (vv.19-20).

He was hoping against all hope somehow, some way, the God of Daniel would rescue him.

By a miracle, Daniel answered, *"O king, live for ever. My God hath sent his angel, and hath shut the lions' mouths, that they have not hurt me: forasmuch as before him innocency was found in me; and also before thee, O king, have I done no hurt"* (vv.21-22).

The delighted ruler had Daniel brought out of the den and there wasn't a scratch on his body.

THE PLOT BACKFIRES

Here's what happened next. The tables were turned against those who plotted against Daniel. The Bible records, *"And the king commanded, and they brought those men which had accused Daniel, and they cast them into the den of lions, them, their children, and their wives; and the lions had the mastery of them, and brake all their bones in pieces or ever they came at the bottom of the den"* (v.24).

It was another "sword of Goliath" moment. Those who prepared the lions to destroy Daniel, were devoured by the lions themselves!

It was another "sword of Goliath" moment.

A NEW DECREE

Because Daniel was faithful to the Lord, the entire nation was spiritually transformed. Darius issued a new edict that must have made the angels in heaven rejoice.

The king *"...wrote unto all people, nations, and languages, that dwell in all the earth; Peace be multiplied unto you. I make a decree, That in every dominion of my kingdom men tremble and fear before the God of Daniel: for he is the living God, and stedfast for ever, and his kingdom that which shall not be destroyed, and his dominion shall be even unto the end. He delivereth and rescueth, and he worketh signs and wonders in heaven and in earth, who hath delivered Daniel from the power of the lions"* (vv.25-27).

IT'S YOUR DECISION

Like Daniel, the impact of your choice can have a far-reaching effect—not only on your immediate circle of friends, but on schools, businesses and even governments and nations.

However, as you learn from living the Christian life, lions don't just live in dens. The Bible tells us, *"Be sober, be vigilant; because your adversary the devil, as a roaring lion, walketh about, seeking whom he may devour"* (1 Peter 5:8).

Resist Satan. Stand firm and you will see God's deliverance.

Have you made the ultimate decision? I pray you can declare, *"...as for me and my house, we will serve the Lord"* (Joshua 24:15).

CHAPTER THREE

THE HANGMAN'S NOOSE

But when Esther came before the king, he commanded by letters that his wicked device, which he devised against the Jews, should return upon his own head, and that he and his sons should be hanged on the gallows.

– ESTHER 9:25

I love the old western films of life in the frontier towns of the wild west—and I still watch them every once in a while on the Classic Movie Channel.

In one plot, a band of crooked cowboys built a hangman's platform on main street in front of the saloon to get rid of one of their enemies—an innocent man. At high noon, they placed the victim's head in the noose and were about to pull the boards from underneath his feet.

Suddenly, the good guys in white hats came riding into town to save the day. At the last possible second, they pull the innocent man to safety and hang the bad guys on the very gallows they built!

THE VANQUISHED QUEEN

There's a true-life parallel to this drama found in the Old Testament.

Our heroine is a young Jewish woman named Esther, an exile in Susa, a city in the land of Persia.

The Bible records how King Ahasuerus, ruler of the empire, threw a huge exhibit of his great wealth. It lasted six months and was completed by a seven-day party where the wine flowed freely.

On the final day, he wanted to impress the guests with the beauty of his wife, Queen Vashti.

But since she was giving a reception for the women of the region that night, she refused to attend. "Why should I parade before his drunken friends," she thought.

The king was so upset with her insolence, he issued a decree: "*That Vashti come no more before king Ahasuerus; and let the king give her royal estate unto another that is better than she*"(Esther 1:16). He was really trying to tell his subjects, "Don't let women tell you what to do."

To find a replacement for the queen, he decided to have a national beauty contest. In Susa there was beautiful girl named Esther—an orphan being raised by her uncle, Mordecai.

"Keep your Jewish heritage a secret."

The uncle convinced her to enter the pageant, "But keep your Jewish heritage a secret." Her ancestors had been brought to the land when Nebuchadnezzar conquered Israel generations earlier.

"GRACE AND FAVOR"

Many young women were chosen to progress into phase two of the competition—and were brought to the palace where they were given beauty treatments in preparation for the time they would meet the king.

Esther won the admiration of everyone who met her, and when she went before Ahasuerus,

> *Esther won the admiration of everyone who met her.*

"...the king loved Esther above all the women, and she obtained grace and favour in his sight more than all the virgins; so that he set the royal crown upon her head, and made her queen instead of Vashti" (Esther 2:17).

A national holiday was proclaimed to celebrate the event.

UNCOVERING A PLOT

Esther secretly kept in contact with Mordecai (whose Jewish heritage was known) by passing notes to him when he would come to the palace gate.

One day, Mordecai overheard a conversation between two of the king's eunuchs who guarded the entrance. They were plotting to kill Ahasuerus.

He immediately sent word to Esther—who in turned informed the king, giving credit to Mordecai. An investigation ensued and the two men were hanged on a gallows. A report of the entire matter was written in a logbook kept for the king's use.

THE EVIL DECREE

Years later, Ahasuerus named a new prime minster for his kingdom. His name was Haman— and he proved to be a wicked man.

Just as the Lord places certain men and women in positions for special missions, Satan promotes people like Nimrod, or even a Hitler, to do his evil work.

Haman was so proud of his title and authority he had the king make a decree that people must bow to him wherever he went. Mordecai, however, refused—and Haman was outraged.

His fury would not be wasted on just one Jew; Haman began plotting to have every person of Hebrew ancestry in the kingdom exterminated.

So he told the king, *"There is a certain people* [the Jews] *scattered abroad and dispersed among the people in all the provinces of thy kingdom; and their laws are diverse from all people; neither keep they the king's laws: therefore it is not for the king" profit to suffer them. If it please the king, let it be written that they may be destroyed: and I will pay ten thousand talents of silver to the hands of those that have the charge of the business, to bring it into the king's treasuries"* (Esther 3:8-9).

Since it was Haman's money, Ahasuerus didn't pay much attention to the request, but signed the decree anyway, saying, "Do whatever you want with those people."

A MASSACRE IN THE MAKING

Haman had bulletins sent to every province in

the land that on the thirteenth day of the twelfth month every Hebrew in Persia was to be killed.

When Mordecai learned of this diabolical plan, he put on sackcloth and ashes and went through the streets crying bitterly. Esther heard of Mordecai's grief and sent one of her assistants out of the palace to give him new clothes—and to find out why he was so outraged.

Mordecai gave the assistant a copy of the bulletin ordering the massacre so it could be shown to Esther. "Please have her intercede for our people," he begged.

Mordecai gave the assistant a copy of the bulletin ordering the massacre so it could be shown to Esther.

When she learned of the edict, Esther sent the messenger back to Mordecai to explain the difficult circumstance she was in—and why she could not barge in and petition Ahasuerus. *"All the king's servants, and the people of the king's provinces, do know, that whosoever, whether man or woman, shall come unto the king into the inner* court, *who is not called, there is one law of his to put him to death, except such to whom the king shall hold out the golden sceptre, that he may live: but I have not been called to come in unto the king these thirty days"* (Esther 4:11).

Mordecai immediately sent another urgent message: "Don't think that just because you live in the palace and are the queen that you are the one Jew who will escape alive. If you stay silent, God will rescue our people by some other means, but you will surely be killed"

Then he sent her this thought-provoking statement: *"..and who knoweth whether thou art come to the kingdom for such a time as this?"* (v.14).

FASTING AND PRAYER

When Esther heard those words, she did something which should be a lesson for all of us. She sent her uncle a note asking every Jew in Susa to fast and pray for the next three days. And she said, *"I also and my maidens will fast likewise; and*

so will I go in unto the king, which is not
according to the law: and if I perish, I perish"
(v.16).

Not only was Esther beautiful, she had great
wisdom—and the Jewish people in the city prayed
earnestly for God's favor on her.

Three days later, Esther, dressed in her royal
robes, stood in the inner court near the entrance
to the king's throne room. God heard her prayer,
because when Ahasuerus saw her, he dipped his
scepter, giving her favor to enter. Remember, if he
had not extended the scepter, Esther could have
been killed for breaking the law and illegally
entering the throne room.

The welcome was more than she expected.
"What is your desire, Queen Esther?" the king
asked. "What do you want?"
Then he added, *"...it shall*
be even given thee to the
half of the kingdom"
(Esther 5:3).

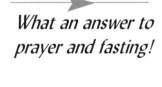

What an answer to
prayer and fasting!

What an answer to prayer and fasting!

BUILDING THE GALLOWS

Esther replied, "If it please the king, I want you to come with Haman to a dinner I have prepared for him."

That evening, during the meal—in the presence of Haman—the king repeated what he had earlier promised Esther: "What is it you want? Half of my kingdom is not too much for you. Just ask."

Esther said, "If you really favor me, I want you and Haman to return for dinner tomorrow night when I will give you my answer."

"I want you and Haman to return for dinner tomorrow night when I will give you my answer."

Haman left the palace proud as a peacock to have been invited for a second night in a row—until he saw Mordecai sitting at the king's gate, ignoring him and once more refusing to bow. When Haman reached his home he gathered his wife and friends around to brag about the royal treatment he was receiving, but he admitted, *"Yet all this availeth me nothing, so long as I see Mordecai the Jew sitting at the king's gate"* (v.13).

Haman's wife and those present had an idea. *"Let a gallows be made of fifty cubits high, and tomorrow speak thou unto the king that Mordecai may be hanged thereon: then go thou in merrily with the king unto the banquet"* (v.14).

The next morning Haman prepared the hangman's gallows.

THE CHRONICLE

That same night—after the first of Esther's two dinners—the king couldn't sleep. So he asked one of his assistants to bring the book which recorded the chronicle of events which had taken place during the 12 years of his reign. They happened to read the account of the time Mordecai had exposed the plot of the two royal eunuchs who had conspired to assassinate the king.

"What great honor was given to Mordecai for this?" Ahasuerus wanted to know.

They replied, *"There is nothing done for him"* (Esther 6:3).

A ROYAL ROBE

When he realized Mordecai had never been properly commended, the king wanted to talk with someone in the palace about making such plans.

The first person he spotted was Haman, who had arrived early, wanting to talk to the king about hanging Mordecai on the gallows he had just built for him.

Before Haman could say a word, the king asked him, *"What shall be done unto the man whom the king delighteth to honour?"* (v.6).

Flattered, Haman thought, "The king must be talking about me"—so he suggested the person be given a royal robe, ride through the city on a king's horse and have a prince announce his arrival (vv.8-9).

MORTIFIED MORDECAI

It must have been the shock of Haman's life when the king ordered, *"Make haste, and take the apparel and the horse, as thou hast said, and do even so to Mordecai the Jew, that sitteth at the king's gate: let nothing fail of all that thou hast spoken"*(v.10).

Devastated, but with no choice in the matter, Haman robed Mordecai, placed him on a horse, and led him through the city, proclaiming, *"Thus shall it be done unto the man whom the king delighteth to honour"*(v.11).

After the procession, Haman was mortified and hid his face, but the king's assistants hurried him to the dinner Esther had prepared.

"WHERE IS HE?"

At this second dinner party, the king repeated his promise: "Queen Esther, what would you like? Just ask—up to half the kingdom."

Esther must have whispered a prayer to heaven before giving her bold answer. She said, *"If I have found favour in thy sight, O king, and if it please the king, let my life be given me at my petition, and my people at my request: For we are sold, I and my people, to be destroyed, to be slain, and to perish"* (Esther 7:3-4).

King Ahasuerus exploded in rage. "Who would tell me to order such a thing? Where is he?"

> *King Ahasuerus exploded in rage.*

Esther pointed across the table, announcing, *"The adversary and enemy is this wicked Haman"* (v.6).

Terror stricken, Haman fell at the feet of Esther and began pleading for his life. Then one of the eunuchs attending the king spoke up: "Look over there," he said, pointing out a window, "There's the gallows Haman built for Mordecai—the man who saved the king's life."

King Ahasuerus ordered, *"Hang him thereon"* (v.9). And that's how Haman died.

"FOR SUCH A TIME AS THIS"

Once more, God turned the weapon prepared by the enemy for the enemy's own destruction. What the devil means for evil, God will use for good:

■ The enemy of bankruptcy may be
   threatening your business, but God will
   bring a financial miracle so you can
   support His work.
■ The enemy of cancer may attack your
   body, but the Great Physician will heal
   you and give you a testimony which
   will transform lives.
■ The enemy of divorce may invade your
   marriage, yet the Lord will repair your
   broken relationship and give you a
   ministry of restoration.

Perhaps you worry, "I have nothing to fight
with?" Don't panic! God will use the weapons of
your enemies to bring about victory.

Like Esther, you have come to the Kingdom for
such a time as this!

CHAPTER FOUR

THE PIT HAS A PURPOSE

The steps of a good man are ordered by the Lord.
– PSALM 37:23

Life is filled with problems, potholes and pits. You can be walking along on top of the world when suddenly you fall into an unexpected trap—an addiction to drugs or pornography, a financial reversal, a alarming doctor's report or a broken relationship.

However, as incredible as it may seem at the time, the setbacks and snares are for a reason. Yes, every pit has a purpose!

"COME FORTH!"

In the last chapter we found Daniel thrown into a pit of lions. But was that his final resting place?

Later we will see what happened to the three Hebrew children when they were tossed into the fiery furnace.

Think about Lazarus. He was pronounced dead, placed in a burial cave with a rock secured over the opening—I guess they didn't want the dead man to escape!

However, that was before Jesus came on the scene and said to the body of the man who had been dead four days, *"Lazarus, come forth"* (John 11:43).

The deceased man was brought out, wrapped from head to toe in graveclothes with a kerchief covering his face. Then Jesus commanded, *"Loose him, and let him go"* (v.44).

Lazarus was alive!

A DEEP SLEEP

God often does His best work when we are in

the dark. This pattern began in the Garden of Eden after the first man was created. Adam enjoyed walking and talking with God—even naming the animals on earth. He wanted to be a part of what was taking place.

God often does His best work when we are in the dark.

But when it was time for God to create a companion for Adam, the Almighty decided to put him in a dark place so he could not see what the Lord was doing. The Bible says the Creator *"...caused a deep sleep to fall upon Adam"* (Genesis 2:21).

In that darkness, he formed the first woman out of Adam's side (v.22).

The next morning, God awakened Adam and beside him lay the most beautiful creature he had ever seen—Eve.

When God pulls the shades over your eyes He is just preparing you for a glorious daytime experience. In the words of the psalmist, *"...weeping may endure for a night, but joy cometh in the morning"* (Psalm 30:5).

A DARK ROOM

Abraham, "the father of nations," had a similar experience. One evening, *"...when the sun was going down, a deep sleep fell upon Abram; and, lo, an horror of great darkness fell upon him"* (Genesis 15:12). Yet, at that same time, *"...the Lord made a covenant with Abram, saying, Unto thy seed have I given this land"* (v.18).

One of the promises of the Almighty was that Abraham would have a son (his seed), but since he was getting up in years and Sarah was still childless, he interfered with God's plan. In a dark room, Abraham lay with Hagar—Sarah's Egyptian handmaiden—and produced a child contrary to God's will. His name was Ishmael, whose descendants populated the Arab world (Genesis 25:12-18) and are still at war in the Middle East today.

When you are going through a deep, dark experience, don't try to rush or change God's plans. Allow Him to finish the work He has started.

Thankfully, Abraham's life got back on track and he and Sarah became the parents of the promised son, Isaac.

THE DREAMER

One of the most powerful stories in the Old Testament concerns Joseph. He was a chosen vessel used to deliver his people from a devastating famine.

If you dare to dream, Satan will often sow discord in your own family.

From his earliest days, Joseph was a dreamer. But when he had a vision of his father, mother and all his brothers bowing down to him (Genesis 37:5-11), his brothers became jealous and began to think about his destruction.

If you dare to dream, Satan will often sow discord in your own family.

His brothers developed such hatred for Joseph that one day they threw him in a literal pit, intending he should die. Yet, God knew where he

63

was all the time.

The Lord arranged for a caravan of traders to pass by, and the brothers sold Joseph for a few pieces of silver.

God knew where he was all the time.

He was taken to Egypt and sold once again to Potiphar a guard of Pharaoh. But when Potiphar's wife tried to seduce Joseph, he was thrown into prison—another dark place.

GOD MEANT IT FOR GOOD

Because of his God-given ability, Joseph was eventually brought before Pharaoh to interpret a perplexing dream. As a result, he was released from prison and became second in command in all of Egypt.

The day finally arrived when, during a great famine in Israel, Joseph's brothers traveled to Egypt to purchase food. Whom did they have to bow before (in fulfillment of the earlier dream)? None other than the brother they had cast in the pit.

Now the situation was reversed. Joseph could easily have had them arrested and sentenced to prison. Instead, he forgave his brothers and gave them sufficient supplies to ease the famine in his homeland. Joseph told them, *"But as for you, ye thought evil against me; but God meant it unto good, to bring to pass, as it is this day, to save much people alive"* (Genesis 50:20).

FROM A TO Z

Satan's pits are real, but never forget there is a reason and purpose for their existence. For example, God didn't place Job in his dire predicament as judgment. No, the Lord knew Job was a righteous man and *allowed* Satan to test him—knowing Job would pass with flying colors.

Your Heavenly Father is fully aware of the oppressive times in your life and He cares just as much for you then as He does in times of victory and rejoicing.

At the cross, Jesus did not pay half price for you, He paid for your sin in *full* with His precious blood.

65

God has an exact plan for your future. He knows where you have been and where you are going. Even if you should stumble into one of Satan's snares, God is watching and is still in control.

The Lord is taking you from point A to point Z, and in between there are going to be a few other letters—for example, some P's (Problems, Persecutions and People) and T's (Trials, Tribulations and Temptations).

Through it all, God promises, *"I will never leave thee, nor forsake thee"* (Hebrews 13:5).

STUMBLING IN THE DARK

I remember the night I was asleep at home when I was awakened by a sudden noise. When I opened my eyes I saw a man standing in our bedroom doorway. Panicked, I screamed, jumped out of bed and flipped on the light.

Guess what? The image I feared was a coat hanging on the door and there was no danger. All I needed was a little illumination!

In our dark times, we often see things that are not really there. As the Bible tells us, *"If a man walketh in the night, he stumbles, because there is no light"* (John 11:10).

God offers us all the brightness we need.

God offers us all the brightness we need. Jesus says, *"I am the light of the world: he that followeth me shall not walk in darkness, but shall have the light of life"* (John 8:12).

Scripture records at the moment Christ died on the cross, the sun turned black and *"...there was a darkness all over the earth"* (Luke 23:44).

Then, after the crucifixion and burial of Jesus, on the third day before daylight—during the darkest part of the night—the stone was rolled away and out walked the brightest light man has ever seen.

THE ROCK

Jesus shared a parable of the wise man who built his house on a rock and the foolish man who built his house on the sand (Matthew 7).

Suddenly, the heavens opened and the rains fell. Both men experienced dark, stormy times, but the wise man knew the secret to survival. *"... the rain descended, and the floods came, and the winds blew, and beat upon that house; and it fell not: for it was founded upon a rock"* (v.25).

> *Both men experienced dark, stormy times, but the wise man knew the secret to survival.*

This solid Rock is Jesus (1 Corinthians 10:4).

THE TABLES WILL BE TURNED

It is when you are in the bleakest circumstance God's light will shine the brightest. In fact, He is waiting right now to bring you out of your night:

- There is no need Jesus can't fulfill.
- There is no sin in your life Jesus cannot forgive.
- There is no infirmity in you body Jesus cannot heal.

Your enemy, Satan, will do everything in his power to throw you into a pit and leave you there. But, thank God, one day soon the tables will be turned. What the devil has used against you from the day you were born will be his own downfall.

Scripture declares, God is going to *"...cast him into the bottomless pit, and shut him up, and set a seal upon him, that he should deceive the nations no more"* (Revelation 20:3).

He will know what true outer darkness looks like!

AN ON-TIME GOD

The same Lord who called, equipped, ordained and anointed you is by your side no matter how deep the hole or how black the night you are facing. He is asking you to *"...stand still, and see the salvation of the Lord"* (Exodus 14:13).

For those who are depressed, oppressed and obsessed, waiting for an answer, remember that we serve an on-time God. He is never early or late—always there at the right moment, according to His perfect will.

Help is Just a Prayer Away

What does it take to lift you out of the negative circumstances in which you may find yourself? It's not your mother, your father, your grandparents, a psychologist, a television preacher or winning the lottery.

Before you were ever conceived, God knew you in your mother's womb and has been watching over you ever since. In fact, He knows the problems you are struggling with at this very moment.

Isn't it time to stop leaning on man and start calling on God? He is:

- Jehovah Jirah—the God who provides.
- Jehovah Shammah—the God who is always there.
- Jehovah Rapha—the God who heals.

The omnipresent Father is with you whether

skies are bright or gloomy.

Why be self-centered, thinking you can solve all your problems alone? It won't work! Humble yourself and admit you need help. Fall on your face before the Lord and cry, "God, please take control of this dark situation. I give my life to you. Take me, shape and mold me and make me into who you want me to be. Lift me out of this place."

With the psalmist you will be able to rejoice: *"He brought me up also out of an horrible pit, out of the miry clay, and set my feet upon a rock, and established my goings"* (Psalm 40:2)

Hallelujah!

CHAPTER FIVE

THE SMELL OF SMOKE

*And the princes, governors, and captains,
and the king's counselors, being gathered
together, saw these men, upon whose bodies the
fire had no power, nor was an hair of their head
singed, neither were their coats changed, nor
the smell of fire [smoke] had passed on them.*
– DANIEL 3:27

Fire! It can be your friend or your enemy. The same flame used to cook your meals can burn your house to the ground and destroy all your possessions. It can melt the impurities out of gold or burn thousands of acres of fertile forest land.

A fire can heat iron ore to the temperature where it can be molded into valuable objects of steel. Or it may erupt as a volcano and turn an entire city into layers of lava.

On Sunday night, October 9, 1871, a cow in Mrs. O'Leary's dairy barn knocked over a lantern and set off the Great Chicago Fire. Within 24 hours 300 died, 90,000 were homeless and the center of the city lay in ashes.

SUFFERING FOR THE SAVIOR

Fire—both for better and for worse—has accompanied the spread of the Gospel.

For example Nero, the emperor of Rome in the first century, was out to exterminate anyone who professed faith in Jesus. He did not just *kill* Christians, he wanted to make them suffer first.

Nero's atrocities included setting believers on fire, marching them through the streets of Rome, and yelling, "Now you truly are the light of the world."

A STATUE OF GOLD

To punish God-fearing people with flames of fire is not anything new. It was used by King Nebuchadnezzar long ago.

After he invaded Israel and brought thousands of slaves back to Babylon, the king had a 90-foot golden statue made of himself. He set it up on a plain near the city of Dura.

To punish God-fearing people with flames is not anything new.

At the dedication ceremony, a royal herald announced in a loud voice: *"To you it is commanded, O people, nations, and languages, that at what time ye hear the sound of the cornet, flute, harp, sackbut, psaltery, dulcimer, and all kinds of music, ye fall down and worship the golden image that Nebuchadnezzar the king hath set up: And whoso falleth not down and worshippeth shall the same hour be cast into the midst of a burning fiery furnace"* (Daniel 3:4-6).

Then, as the band began to play, everyone present—regardless of race, color or creed—fell down before the golden idol and began to worship.

EXTREME PRESSURE

Well, not everyone bowed! There were three Hebrew men present who refused to obey. You'll recognize their names, Shadrach, Meshach and Abdednego. These were the same Jews who had been hand-chosen and trained at the king's palace (along with Daniel) to become leaders in Babylon. By this time they had risen to high positions in the kingdom.

They had been under extreme pressure to abandon their faith in the God Jehovah.

Of course, they had been under extreme pressure to abandon their faith in the God Jehovah.

"IS IT TRUE?"

Immediately, there were people who noticed how the three Hebrews refused to fall to their knees and bow to the statue. They delighted in telling Nebuchadnezzar, *"...these men, O king, have not regarded thee: they serve not thy gods, nor worship the golden image which thou hast set up"* (v.12).

The king was furious! He called the three in and asked "Is it true that you do not honor my gods and defy the decree to worship this golden idol I have erected?"

However, he gave them one last chance, saying, "If you don't bow the next time you hear the music, I will have no other option but to throw you into the burning furnace." Then he asked, *"...and who is that God that shall deliver you out of my hands?"* (v.15).

This was not only a challenge to the three Hebrew men, but to the Almighty Himself. What a terrible mistake!

No Compromise

These young men didn't need a council meeting to decide what to do. They knew who they were and what they stood for.

Perhaps you are facing a fire at this moment.

You may even feel you are already in the furnace and the flames are licking at your feet. The pressure is on at work or an inferno is raging in your family.

In our stress-filled world, our fiery furnaces come in the form of our schools, our jobs and our finances. The world is asking us to compromise and bow to the carnality of the culture. They say, "Everyone else is doing it, why not you?"

It takes holy boldness to stand firm in the face of such pressure.

The three Hebrews had family members in Babylon, yet they didn't care how others responded to the king's orders. These men were not going to bend and bow to an idol made by man.

Having a relationship with God is not about your church or you family—it is one-on-one, between you and the Lord.

Seven Times Hotter!

Shadrach, Meshach and Abednego, steadfast in

their faith, gave this answer to the king: *"O Nebuchadnezzar, we are not careful to answer thee in this matter. If it be so, our God whom we serve is able to deliver us from the burning fiery furnace, and he will deliver us out of thine hand, O king. But if not, be it known unto thee, O king, that we will not serve thy gods, nor worship the golden image which thou hast set up"* (vv.16-18).

What Faith!

The king's anger grew even more intense.

The king's anger grew even more intense. So much so that he *"...commanded that they should heat the furnace...seven times more than it was wont to be heated"* (v.19).

Next. He ordered his strong guards to tie the three men up—by their hands and feet. Then, fully dressed, these godly men were thrown into the blazing fire.

The flames coming out of the furnace were so hot, the soldiers who carried out this act were incinerated in the process.

THE FOURTH MAN

When the heat subsided enough for the king to take a look into the flames, he viewed a scene which shook the entire kingdom of Babylon. An alarmed Nebuchadnezzar exclaimed, *"Did not we cast three men bound into the midst of the fire?"* (v.24). His assistants responded, "That is correct, O king."

Then the sovereign ruler of Babylon announced, *"Lo, I see four men loose, walking in the midst of the fire, and they have no hurt; and the form of the fourth is like the Son of God"* (v.25).

Jesus was in the fire, protecting those three loyal men of faith.

Jesus was in the fire, protecting those three loyal men of faith.

"BUT IF NOT"

Friend, just when you think the flames will engulf you, if you refuse to yield to the coercion of this world, Almighty God will show up.

To Shadrach, Meshach and Abednego, there

was no doubt their God could and *would* deliver them, "but if not" they were going to serve Jehovah anyway. Job expressed the same determination when it looked as if the end was near. He declared, *"Though he slay me, yet will I trust in him"* (Job 13:15).

Will this be your testimony? Are you ready to keep your covenant with the Lord *regardless* of the trials and tests you endure?

MORE THAN CONQUERORS

If you know Jesus as your Savior, there is a part of you that cannot be destroyed. Despite the crisis you face, you are able to say with the apostle Paul, *"Who shall separate us from the love of Christ? shall tribulation, or distress, or persecution, or famine, or nakedness, or peril, or sword?...Nay, in all these things we are more than conquerors through him that loved us. For I am persuaded, that neither death, nor life, nor angels, nor principalities, nor powers, nor things present, nor things to come, nor height, nor depth, nor any other creature, shall be able to separate us from the love of God, which is in Christ Jesus our Lord"* (Romans 8:35,37-39).

No demon in hell can pluck you out of the hand of God and nothing can touch the Holy Spirit who lives inside you. Why? Because, *"...greater is he that is in you, than he that is in the world"* (1 John 4:4).

God is not afraid of the fire—after all, He created it! And He is not frightened by your situation, your trials or your troubles. He says, *"...I will never leave thee, nor forsake thee"* (Hebrews 13:5).

No Singe—No Smell

When King Nebuchadnezzar saw the four men walking around in the flames, he came near the furnace and ordered them to come out.

Shadrach, Meshach and Abednego were walking around like nothing was happening! They were in no hurry to leave because when you are in the presence of the Lord and He is walking by your side, you want to stay in that place forever!

The atmosphere changes when God shows up.

These three Hebrews had to be *ordered* by the king to leave the furnace. And when they did, all the

The atmosphere changes when God shows up.

princes, counselors and government leaders gathered around to examine them. They found the men, *"...upon whose bodies the fire had no power, nor was an hair of their head singed, neither were their coats changed, nor the smell of fire had passed on them"* (27).

You will never be the same when God walks with you in the midst of your crisis.

THE INCENSE OF GOD

Perhaps you have suffered through a terrible situation. It's time to release every negative thought concerning your yesterday...even the "odor" or stench of your rotten past.

When God delivers you from the inferno, there is no smell of smoke left on your body! The apostle Paul tells us that we should give forth *"...a sweet smell, a sacrifice acceptable, well pleasing to God"* (Philippians 4:8). The incense of the Father should flow from our very being.

What is the lingering smell of smoke? It is:

- Saying, "I have forgiven them, but I'll never forget what they did to me."
- The fact you were hurt 10 or 20 years ago and still talk about the matter.
- Feeling anger and hatred toward another person.
- Harboring resentment or jealousy.

Once God has walked with you and has brought you out, there is no reason to remain bitter over your circumstances. The Lord will cleanse you and set you free.

I've met many believers who have suffered through fiery trials but you would never know it. Why? Because, with God's help, they refused to allow the scent of the situation to remain. They were totally restored.

A NEW DECREE

Nebuchadnezzar became a changed man because of the miracle he witnessed. He declared, *"Blessed be the God of Shadrach, Meshach, and Abednego, who hath sent his angel, and delivered his servants that trusted in him, and have changed the*

> *Nebuchadnezzar became a changed man because of the miracle he witnessed.*

king's word, and yielded their bodies, that they might not serve nor worship any god, except their own God" (Daniel 3:28).

This heathen ruler learned in a hurry! Immediately, he made this decree: *"That every people, nation, and language, which speak any thing amiss against the God of Shadrach, Meshach, and Abednego, shall be cut in pieces, and their houses shall be made a dunghill: because there is no other God that can deliver after this sort"* (v.29).

Instead of cursing the living God, the king was now praising Him, saying, *"How great are his signs! and how mighty are his wonders!"* (Daniel 4:3).

Because of their unbending faith, the three Hebrews were promoted to even higher responsibilities in Babylon.

THE ONLY FIRE YOU NEED

Satan is only fooling himself when he attempts to confine you in a cauldron of crisis and crank up the heat! The very flame he ignites will be his final destruction. The Bible says, *"And the devil that deceived them was cast into the lake of fire and brimstone, where the beast and the false prophet are, and shall be tormented day and night for ever and ever"* (Revelation 20:10).

Friend, the only fire you need to seek is the one first prophesied by John the Baptist. He declared, *"I indeed baptize you with water unto repentance: but he that cometh after me is mightier than I, whose shoes I am not worthy to bear: he shall baptize you with the Holy Ghost, and with fire"* (Matthew 3:11).

Just before Jesus returned to the Father, He promised to send the Holy Spirit—who descended at the Upper Room. The Bible says, *"And there appeared unto them cloven tongues like as of fire, and it sat upon each of them"* (Acts 2:3).

I pray you have welcomed this fire from above into your life.

CHAPTER SIX

AN ISSUE
OF BLOOD

And a certain woman, which had an issue
of blood twelve years, and had suffered many
things of many physicians, and had spent all that
she had, and was nothing bettered, but rather grew
worse. When she had heard of Jesus, came in the
press behind, and touched his garment. For she
said, If I may touch but his clothes, I shall be
whole. And straightway the fountain of her
blood was dried up; and she felt in her body
that she was healed of that plague.

– MARK 5:25-29

B lood is the river of life. This red fluid,
pumped by the heart into your arteries and veins,

carries oxygen and cell-building materials which sustains your existence. It also carries the heritage—"the blood line"—of your family.

A Cover for Guilt

In the very first book of the Bible, we find God using blood as an atonement for sin.

We know the story of how Adam and Eve disobeyed the Lord by eating of the fruit of the forbidden tree. Before that time, *"...they were both naked...and were not ashamed"* (Genesis 2:25).

> In the very first book of the Bible, we find God using blood as an atonement for sin.

Because of the shame of their transgression, *"...the eyes of them both were opened, and they knew that they were naked; and they sewed fig leaves together, and made themselves aprons"* (Genesis 3:7). It was man's way of covering his guilt.

However, from the beginning, God had another plan for atonement for sin—and it involved the shedding of blood. Scripture tells us, *"Unto Adam* also and to his wife did the Lord God make coats of skins, and clothed them" (v.21). In other words, the Almighty had to take the life of an animal to provide a covering for the guilt of their transgressions.

Scripture tells us, "For the life of the flesh is in the blood: and I have given it to you upon the altar to make an atonement for your souls: for it is the blood that maketh an atonement for the soul" (Leviticus 17:11).

The issue is an issue of blood.

BLOOD COVENANTS

Throughout the Bible, God emphasizes the importance of blood—in both sacrifices and covenants:

- The first act of Noah after the flood was to offer a sacrifice to the Lord. He "...took of every clean beast, and of every clean fowl, and offered burnt offerings on the altar" (Genesis 8:20).

91

- Every male in the seed of Abraham was brought into the covenant through the blood of circumcision (Genesis 17:10).
- After Moses first read the Ten Commandments to the children of Israel, they made a peace offering of animals, and *"Moses took the blood, and sprinkled it on the people, and said, Behold the blood of the covenant, which the Lord hath made with you concerning all these words"* (Exodus 24:8).

On a human level, blood covenants are part of world history and are still practiced today in parts of Africa, Asia, South America and the Middle East. Two individuals will cut their wrists and intermingle their blood, making them "blood brothers" until death.

IT SPEAKS!

As amazing as it may seem, the Bible tells us

that blood has a voice—and can actually speak. After Cain killed his brother, Abel, God said to him, *"What hast thou done? the voice of thy brother's blood crieth unto me from the ground"* (Genesis 4:10). Abel's blood screamed out for justice to be served.

Abel's blood screamed out for justice to be served.

However, God did not intend for blood to be a means of destruction, rather it is for our protection. He demonstrated this during the time of the plagues which descended on Pharaoh and the Egyptians.

In the tenth plague, when the death angel came to kill all the firstborn in the land, the houses on which the blood of a lamb was smeared on the doorposts were spared. God told the Israelites, *"...when I see the blood, I will pass over you"* (Exodus 12:13).

It was their covering—and it is still ours today. You and I can pray for the blood of Jesus to protect and save our families. As Paul and Silas said to the keeper of the prison, *"Believe on the Lord Jesus*

Christ, and thou shalt be saved, and thy house" (Acts 16:31)

PRONOUNCED CLEAN!

Not only is blood our atonement and our protection, it is also our cleansing agent.

Again and again in Leviticus and Deuteronomy we see the priests using the blood of bulls, goats or birds to sprinkle over the people for cleansing.

Not only is blood our atonement and our protection, it is also our cleansing agent.

For a leper to be made pure, God's representative *"...shall sprinkle upon him that is to be cleansed from the leprosy seven times, and shall pronounce him clean"* (Leviticus 14:7).

The leper was then returned to the camp.

As a purification for sin, the people were to slaughter *"...a red heifer without spot, wherein is no blemish"* (Numbers 19:2). And *"the priest shall take of her* [the heifer's] *blood with his finger, and sprinkle of her blood directly before the tabernacle of the congregation seven times"* (v.4).

THE SAVIOR BLED

This is a prophetic vision of what Jesus did for you and me on the cross. In this same way you are purified by the blood of Jesus—declared clean and ready to enter God's Kingdom.

Why seven times? The blood of Jesus was shed for you from seven places in His body:

1. From His sweat.

"And being in an agony he prayed more earnestly: and his sweat was as it were great drops of blood falling down to the ground" (Luke 22:44).

2. From His face.

Isaiah prophesied how they plucked out His beard and spat upon Him (Isaiah 50:6).

3. From His head.

They forced a crown of thorns upon His head,

95

and mocking, said, *"Hail, King of the Jews!"* (Matthew 27:29).

4. From His back.

They scourged His back until there was little skin left. He took these 39 stripes for our healing. *"But he was wounded for our transgressions, he was bruised for our iniquities: the chastisement of our peace was upon him; and with his stripes we are healed"* (Isaiah 53:5).

5. From His hands.

As they nailed Christ to the cross, His blood flowed as they pierced His hands (Psalm 22:16).

6. From His feet.

At Calvary, the Roman soldiers pounded nails into His feet (Psalm 22:16).

7. From His side.

The Bible records, *"...one of the soldiers with a*

spear pierced his side, and forthwith came there out blood and water" (John 19:34).

Jesus bled for us as the ultimate sacrifice. By believing on Him, our sins are washed clean and we are ready to enter His Kingdom.

HER LAST HOPE

A woman came to Jesus who had been sick for twelve years with the same problem: it was an issue of blood and the hemorrhaging would not stop.

She had been to many doctors and spent all her money trying to get well, but it was to no avail. Since she was considered "unclean," she could not enter the temple or even shop at the marketplace. The woman was going to die alone and poor—with no one to help her.

The woman was going to die alone and poor—with no one to help her.

Then she heard about a Man named Jesus. Some said He had the spirit of Elijah; others spoke of

Him as the coming Messiah. Friends had told her that as Jesus walked through a village many would be healed.

This was her last hope. The woman had tried everything she knew to be made whole, and Jesus was going to be in her city that very day. She said, "I'm going to find Him!"

The first step to being healed is always to find Jesus.

The first step to being healed is always to find Jesus.

JUST ONE TOUCH

A large crowd had gathered, but a man by the name of Jairus fell at the feet of the Lord, begging Him to go with him to his home because his twelve-year-old daughter was about to die. It was his only child.

Jesus, in His mercy, decided to go with the man and they were making their way through the crowd.

In that scene, the woman with the issue of blood slipped in from behind and reached out to touch the hem of Jesus' robe. She said to herself, *"If I may but touch his garment, I shall be whole"* (Matthew 9:21). Notice, she didn't say "I may be healed," but "I *shall.*"

Her faith was rewarded. Instantly, the woman was healed (Luke 8:44).

HE FELT HER FAITH

At that very moment, Jesus stopped His procession toward the home of Jairus and asked, "Who touched Me?"

When no one stepped forward, Peter, said, *"Master, the multitude throng thee and press thee, and sayest thou, Who touched me? And Jesus said, Somebody hath touched me: for I perceive that virtue is gone out of me"* (vv.45-46).

Jesus said these words because He felt power discharging from His body. He literally felt her faith.

When this woman knew she could not remain hidden, *"...she came trembling, and falling down before him, she declared unto him before all the people for what cause she had touched him, and how she was healed immediately"* (v.47).

Jesus assured her, *"Daughter, be of good comfort: thy faith hath made thee whole; go in peace"* (v.48).

This same Jesus is still healing today!

WONDER WORKING POWER

Let me share four reasons there is such divine power in the blood of Jesus:

First: It is through the blood our sins are forgiven.

Nothing you have done in this life made you a sinner. Because of Adam's fall, you are born in this condition. *"For all have sinned, and come short of the glory of God"* (Romans 3:23).

We enter this world in need of a blood transfusion—which is provided by Christ.

Jesus was sent to earth by the Father to die on the cross and His blood became the remission for your iniquity. We are redeemed, *"...with the precious blood of Christ, as of a lamb without blemish and without spot"* (1 Peter 1:19).

Second: The blood of Jesus will break Satan's hold over your life.

The devil comes to steal, kill and destroy. He will do his best to bind you in sin and attempt to convince you that you belong to him.

The father of lies will try to deceive you into thinking you will die of an incurable disease—or even that you were born a homosexual and cannot change. Don't listen to the deceiver because he has no legal hold on you.

Don't listen to the deceiver because he has no legal hold on you.

When Satan attacks, rebuke him and plead the blood of Christ and watch him flee. It is the strongest weapon you have against the devil.

Third. We can receive the very presence of God through the blood of Jesus.

Scripture tells us we do not enter into the

presence of the Lord through our goodness, but according to the righteousness of Christ. And this comes through His shed blood.

Where is Jesus at this moment? He is in heaven, seated at the right hand of the Father, in the Holy of Holies. And here is how we have access to His presence: *"Having therefore, brethren, boldness to enter into the holiest by the blood of Jesus"* (Hebrews 10:19).

Fourth: We are made complete by the blood of Jesus.

Your entire being can be made whole through the precious blood of the Lamb.

We have this assurance: *"Now the God of peace, that brought again from the dead our Lord Jesus, that great shepherd of the sheep, through the blood of the everlasting covenant, make you perfect in every good work to do his will, working in you that which is well pleasing in his sight, through Jesus Christ"* (Hebrews 13:20-21).

THE REAL ISSUE

The blood is not something to be afraid of, to shun or ignore. Every day we see and hear how Satan attempts to see the world destroyed by the shedding of human blood through violence, murder and war.

However, the blood provided by the Son of God produces an entirely different outcome. It is our link to salvation and eternal life.

Which will you choose?

The issue is an issue of blood!

CHAPTER SEVEN

YOUR WORDS ARE WEAPONS

And they overcame him by the blood of the Lamb, and by the word of their testimony; and they loved not their lives unto the death.

– REVELATION 12:11

Whatever happend to personal honor, when a man's word was his bond—when there was no need for lawyers or a written contract. If an individual told you his intentions, you could count on him. If he said, "Yes" he *meant* "Yes." You didn't have to worry or question.

The Bible tells us, *"...let your yea be yea; and your nay, nay"* (James 5:12).

"GOD SAID"

At creation, two important events happened. First, we read that God the Holy Spirit *"moved"* on the face of the waters (Genesis 1:2). From that moment forward, the Creator *spoke* the world into existence:

- God *said*: *"Let there be light"* (v.3).
- God *said*: *"Let there be a firmament in the midst of the waters..."* (v.6).
- God *said*: *"Let the waters under the heaven be gathered...and let the dry land appear"* (v.9).
- God *said*: *"Let the earth bring forth grass, the herb yielding seed, and the fruit tree..."* (v.11).
- God *said*: "Let [lights]...*divide the day from the night"* (v.14).
- God *said*: *"Let the waters bring forth abundantly..."* (v.20).
- God *said*: *"Let the earth bring forth the living creature..."* (v.24).

■ God *said*: *"Let us make man in our image, after our likeness..."* (v.26).

YOUR DECLARATION

It was through the spoken Word of the Creator that a formless, dark void became a world of substance, light and beauty.

The first chapter of Genesis concludes with these words: *"And God saw every thing that he had made, and, behold, it was very good"* (v.31).

What did the Almighty *see?* All He had *said!* There is miraculous power in the Word!

Since God formed man and woman (v.27) into His own image and changed the face of the earth by speaking, He also expects His children to create good out of bad. How? By speaking His Word!

There is miraculous power in the Word!

You can transform your desolate situation into one that is life-giving, meaningful and beneficial by declaring what He has already spoken.

The Tree Died!

Walking with the disciples one morning on a road near Bethany, Jesus became hungry. In the distance was a fig tree in full bloom, but when they drew closer, He found nothing but leaves —there were no figs. So the Lord pronounced a curse over it: *"No man eat fruit of thee hereafter for ever"* (Mark 11:14).

About twenty-four hours later, when they were returning from Jerusalem on the exact same road, the disciples saw the fig tree—but now it was lifeless and dead. Then Peter, remembering what had happened the previous morning, exclaimed,

> *The Master spoke to the tree and it shriveled and died!*

"Master, behold, the fig tree which thou cursedst is withered away" (v.21).

The Master simply spoke to the tree and it shriveled and died!

"Say Unto This Mountain"

Jesus used the example to teach His disciples a

lesson on faith and belief. He told them, *"...Have faith in God. For verily I say unto you, That whosoever shall say unto this mountain, Be thou removed, and be thou cast into the sea; and shall not doubt in his heart, but shall believe that those things which he saith shall come to pass; he shall have whatsoever he saith. Therefore I say unto you, What things soever ye desire, when ye pray, believe that ye receive them, and ye shall have them"* (Mark 11:22-24).

These verses hold a great truth. Read them again and you'll find the words "say" or "saith" are used repeatedly which indicates the power in the spoken Word.

So don't be surprised when you speak in faith to your problem—your mountain—and there are positive results. Remember, when God completed His creation, He declared, *"...it was very good"* (Genesis 1:31).

"WOE IS ME"

Your enemy will attempt to break your resolve

with words of despair and destruction. Satan will subtly inject doubt, suggesting:

- "You are a nobody and will never succeed."
- "You are sick and will never get well."
- "You are poor and will always stay that way."
- "Nobody really cares about you—and never will."

You are the devil's primary audience—and he delights in telling you these dreadful falsehoods. Sadly, if you listen long enough, uncertainty creeps in and you will likely be saying, "Woe is me." "I'm lost." "I can't win." "I'm no good."

Next, because what you speak comes to pass, your statements become self-fulfilling prophecies. You soon take on the character of the defeated person Satan tricks you into believing you are. You have aided and abetted the process because of the power of your own tongue!

When the devil attempts to confuse you with his litany of lies, remind him where he is headed—cast into a burning hell forever.

There will be a major role reversal. The cat is going to become the mouse! That roaring, prowling lion who seeks whom he may devour, is going be put in a cage from which he will never escape.

The cat is going to become the mouse!

VICTORY IS YOURS!

It's time to open your mouth and declare who you are in Jehovah God.

- "I am fearfully and wonderfully made" (Psalm 139:14).
- "I am a child of God" (John 1:12).
- "I am a member of Christ's body" (Ephesians 5:30).
- "I am the righteousness of God" (2 Corinthians 5:21).
- "I am the head and not the tail!" (Deuteronomy 28:13).

- "I am more than a conqueror through Christ" (Romans 8:37).
- "I am a temple of the Holy Ghost and God's Spirit dwells in me" (1 Corinthians 3:16).
- "I am part of a chosen generation, a royal priesthood" (1 Peter 2:9,10).
- "I am triumphant in Christ Jesus" (2 Corinthians 2:14).
- "I am blessed with all spiritual blessings in heavenly places" (Ephesians 1:3).
- "I am a citizen of heaven" (Philippians 3:20).
- "I am a joint-heir with Christ" (Romans 8:17).
- "I am blessed" (Deuteronomy 28:1-6).

These are not pie-in-the-sky wishes, rather declarations of the Word. Today, don't be ashamed to proclaim to the world that Jesus has won the battle and victory is already yours.

THE PATTERN

The mighty Word of God, plus *your* word of confirmation is an awesome combination. It is the key to your redemption. Scripture tells us, *"...if thou shalt confess with thy mouth the Lord Jesus, and shalt believe in thine heart that God hath raised him from the dead, thou shalt be saved.For with the heart man believeth unto righteousness; and with the mouth confession is made unto salvation"* (Romans 10:9-10).

Confess it!
Say it!
Believe it!

Confess it! Say it! Believe it!

These verses are not only talking about being saved, but apply to any situation you may be facing. The pattern is established and all you have to do is follow.

PREPARATION FOR TESTING

In the beginning of Jesus' ministry, He was baptized in the river Jordan by John. In that divine moment, when He rose up out of the water, the

Holy Spirit descended on Him and God spoke these words from heaven: *"Thou art my beloved Son, in whom I am well pleased"* (Mark 1:11).

Just after this experience, *"Jesus being full of the Holy Ghost returned from Jordan, and was led by the Spirit into the wilderness"* (Luke 4:1).

I pray you have asked the Spirit to lead you in *all* your ways—including a time of testing.

"It Is Written"

During His wilderness experience, the devil tempted Jesus continually for forty day. After this time of fasting, when Jesus was hungry, Satan seized the opportunity to tempt Him even further.

What tactics did the devil use? Just words.

How could Jesus resist this relentless temptation? You say, "He was God's Son, and could withstand any pressure.

What tactics did the devil use?

This is true, yet He was born of a woman and *"...was in all points tempted like as we are"* (Hebrews 4:15).

114

So what did Jesus use to combat the enemy? The devil used words, but the Lord spoke *God's* divine Word! He literally quoted scriptures to confront Satan.

In the first test, the devil said, "Since you are the Son of God, why don't you command this stone to become a loaf of bread?"

Jesus answered, *"It is written, That man shall not live by bread alone, but by every word of God"* (Luke 4:4).

TWO MORE TEMPTATIONS

Next, Satan led Jesus to the peak of a high mountain and showed Him the kingdoms of the world. Then he said, "I'm in charge of all of this, and will turn it over to you if you worship me."

Once more, Jesus answered with the Word, saying, *"Get thee behind me, Satan: for it is written, Thou shalt worship the Lord thy God, and him only shalt thou serve"* (v.8).

For the final test, the devil took Jesus to Jerusalem, to the top of the Temple. Then he suggested, "If you are truly the Son of God, go ahead and jump. Doesn't it say in scripture that angels will catch you, and you won't even dash your foot against a stone?"

Jesus looked at the devil and told him, *"It is said, Thou shalt not tempt the Lord thy God"* (v.12).

At the sound of the Word, the devil retreated.

Have you memorized enough scriptures to use as a powerful weapon against Satan the next time he comes against you? Boldly declare them and he will flee!

"DELIVER US FROM EVIL"

One afternoon a woman in Detroit, Michigan, went grocery shopping. When she returned home, she carried the items from her car to the kitchen.

After putting the groceries away, she walked upstairs to change her clothes, when she suddenly remembered she hadn't locked the back door.

As she started to leave the room to go back down the stairway, a man quickly grabbed her and threw her down on the bed. Placing a knife to her throat, he told her he was going to rape and then kill her. He began to tear off her clothes.

In this crisis moment, the Holy Spirit brought scriptures to the remembrance of this frightened woman.

Verses from the Word came streaming into her mind so quickly that she began quoting them out loud to her assailant. She started with 23rd Psalm: *"The Lord is my shepherd, I shall not want."* And when she reached the part where it says, *"Yea, though I walk through the valley of the shadow of death, I will fear no evil...(v.4),* the potential rapist jumped to his feet and screamed "Stop it!"

> He dropped the knife, covered his ears and yelled, "Stop saying that!"

He dropped the knife, covered his ears and yelled "Stop saying that!"

"THAT'S HER!"

She knew the tables had turned, so she began quoting the psalm again, plus other verses. The agitated intruder backed up, right down the stairs—and she bravely followed him, still quoting God's Word.

He ran out the back door and fled into the street while she began to cry and praise God at the same time, thankful He had "delivered her from evil" (see Matthew 6:13).

Quickly locking the door, she called the police. When they arrived at her house about 30 minutes later, they had a handcuffed man in their custody. When she went outside to identify him, he began to scream "That's her, that's her! She's the lady who beat me up—who tried to kill me."

The woman looked at him in disbelief and couldn't believe her eyes. He was beaten and bloody from head to toe. His clothes were torn and it looked as if he had been whip-lashed before surrendering to the police.

No one will ever know what really happened in this amazing incident, but the woman learned first-hand there is power in the Word of God.

DON'T RUN AND HIDE

Just as Jesus used the Word to defeat Satan, you can too. Never forget what David shouted to Goliath, *"Thou comest to me with a sword, and with a spear, and with a shield: but I come to thee in the name of the Lord of hosts"* (1 Samuel 17:45).

Those words are just as effective today as when the young shepherd boy spoke them long ago.

When your enemies come against you, don't run and hide. Declare God's Word!

CHAPTER EIGHT

IT IS FINISHED!

Which none of the princes of this
world knew: For had they known it, they would
not have crucified the Lord of Glory.
— I CORINTHIANS 2 : 8

Have you ever done something and a few days later, said to yourself, "Why in the world did I ever do such a stupid thing?"

Yes, I have—and I'm sure you are guilty too. We have all made terrible mistakes and because we didn't have a foreknowledge of the results, we regretted ever taking such action.

Some errors can never be erased from our memory and will haunt us until eternity.

Just the Beginning!

Satan found himself in this same predicament. He plotted, planned and schemed to have Jesus arrested and found guilty. When the Son of God was nailed to the cross at Calvary and pronounced dead, he rubbed his hands in glee, thinking the battle was over.

Little did the devil know that the cross was just the beginning! He did not understand the plan of God—which was later revealed to the apostles.

Remember, Satan is not an all-knowing creature. As a fallen angel he no longer had access to the divine plan of heaven and now works through disobedient men and women to fulfill his evil purposes.

"Hidden" Wisdom

The fact the devil had no prior knowledge of God's plan of redemption was made clear by the apostle Paul, who told the believers at Corinth, *"...my preaching was not with enticing words of man's wisdom, but in demonstration of the Spirit"*

(1 Corinthians 2:4). Then he added that he did not declare the *"...wisdom of this world, nor of the princes of this world* [Satan and his demons], *that come to nought. But we speak the wisdom of God in a mystery, even the hidden wisdom, which God ordained before the world unto our glory"* (vv.6-7).

What was this "hidden" understanding? It was God's ultimate plan of salvation— *"Which none of the princes* [devils] *of this world knew: for had they known it, they would not have crucified the Lord of glory"* (1 Corinthians 2:8).

What was this "hidden" understanding?

The fullness of this mystery was not revealed until the resurrection. The principalities, powers of darkness and authorities of the unseen world—and Satan Himself—had no idea Jesus would rise from the tomb.

WHERE WAS JESUS?

Even the disciples, who had been side by side

with the Master during his three years of ministry—were in shock and disbelief that Christ was not dead, but alive.

When Mary Magdalene, Joanna, Mary the mother of James and other women came to the tomb carrying burial spices and discovered the stone rolled back and no sign of Christ's body, they were perplexed. Then two men (angels) appeared and said, *"Why seek ye the living among the dead? He is not here, but is risen: remember how he spake unto you when he was yet in Galilee, saying, The Son of man must be delivered into the hands of sinful men, and be crucified, and the third day rise again. And they remembered his words"* (Luke 24:5-8).

Immediately, the women rushed to share the news with the disciples, but *"...their words seemed to them as idle tales, and they believed them not"* (v.11).

HE WAS THERE

That same day, two men were walking on the

road to Emmaus, expressing their sadness at the loss of Jesus. Then suddenly, He appeared and began walking along side them, but they did not recognize Him (v.16).

"What are you discussing that grieves you so?" asked the Lord.

They answered, *"Art thou only a stranger in Jerusalem, and hast not known the things which are come to pass there in these days?"* (v.18).

> "What are you discussing that grieves you so?"

"What things?" asked Christ.

They told Him the story of what happened to Jesus at Calvary—still not knowing He was in their presence.

He reminded them of what the prophets had foretold about the Messiah. That evening He even had supper with them. And the moment they finally recognized it was truly Jesus, He disappeared (v.31).

THE EVIDENCE

That night they ran to Jerusalem to tell the

disciples what they had witnessed. While they were talking, suddenly Jesus appeared and said "Peace be with you."

The disciples *"...were terrified and affrighted, and supposed that they had seen a spirit"* (v.37).

Jesus asked them, *"Why are ye troubled? and why do thoughts arise in your hearts? Behold my hands and my feet, that it is I myself: handle me, and see; for a spirit hath not flesh and bones, as ye see me have"* (vv.38-39). He showed them the evidence—the nail scars in His hands and feet.

Only then did their thoughts travel back to what He had said at the Last Supper: *"But after I am risen again, I will go before you into Galilee"* (Matthew 26:32).

They had heard His words, but the possibility of a literal resurrection was too much for their human minds to register or comprehend.

Yet Jesus was alive! And the disciples were filled with great joy. You could find them in the temple, *"...praising and blessing God"* (Luke 24:53).

THE SWORD OF GOLIATH

A Painful Death

Jesus came to this earth to be obedient to the will of the Father—which included the cross.

The Romans had learned the art of crucifixion well. It was used to punish and kill criminals, and as a deterrent to keep the people in the lands they captured in line. At times they would nail a

> *The Romans had learned the art of crucifixion well.*

man to a cross and place it on a busy street corner for all to see—spreading fear into the hearts of their subjects.

Soldiers from Rome knew how to make a victim suffer in excruciating pain and agony until his diaphragm would fail and he could no longer breathe. They would break the person's legs so he couldn't push upward to snatch a fresh breath of air.

The cross was a horrible way to die and the Romans crucified thousands of Jews in this brutal fashion while they ruled Israel.

A NEW ERA

Hebrew history tells us that a Roman general by the name of Titus (not the same Titus who worked with Paul at Ephesus), crucified so many Jews in Jerusalem, they ran out of wood for crosses and out of space to place them in the ground around the walls of Jerusalem. Titus killed as many as 500 this way in one day!

So, to the Romans soldiers, nailing Jesus to the cross meant nothing—it was a normal day for them. They had no idea this was the dividing point in world history, and their own calendars would one day be marked by that day on Golgotha: B.C. (Before Christ) and A.D.(After Death).

They had no idea this was the dividing point in world history.

IN ONE ACCORD

As incredible as it may seem, on the day Christ was hung on the cross there was universal agreement that He must die.

Look for a moment at what Jesus had earlier

taught: *"That if two of you shall agree on earth as touching any thing that they shall ask, it shall be done for them of my Father which is in heaven"* (Matthew 18:19).

In Genesis 1, it was God, the Holy Spirit and Jesus who agreed the world should be formed (v.2). Remember, Jesus was present because *"In the beginning was the Word..."* (John 1:1), *"And the Word was made flesh, and dwelt among us"* (v.14). That Word was Jesus.

Because the Father, Son and Holy Spirit always agree, light appears and beauty rises from ashes.

IS IT GOD'S WILL?

Eleven chapters later in Genesis we read of the Tower of Babel. Men who were created in the image of God united to build a structure *"...whose top may reach unto heaven"* (Genesis 11:4).

No cranes of steel, no bulldozers, no cement trucks or even scaffolds. Just a group of people who were all in agreement. About them, God said, *"Behold, the people is one, and they have all one language; and this they begin to do: and now nothing will be restrained from them, which they have imagined to do"* (v.6).

> The power of agreement only ultimately succeeds when it is part of God's will.

However, the power of agreement only ultimately succeeds when it is part of God's will. At Babel, it was all man's decision, so what did the Lord do? He confounded their languages and scattered the people across the earth (vv.7-8).

SOMETHING IN COMMON

Remember, on the day Jesus was crucified everyone was in agreement that He must die:

- The Pharisees, Sadducees, and Jewish leaders wanted Him dead because He was a threat to their teachings.
- The Romans pushed to get rid of Him because He was undermining their authority.

- Satan and all His demons said, "We know He is the Son of God and we must kill Him if we are to totally control the world.
- Finally, God Himself planned that Jesus must die. Just before Christ went to the cross, He said, *"...my will, but thine, be done"* (Luke 22:42). God did not send Jesus to condemn the world, "...but that the world through him might be saved (John 3:17). This required the ultimate sacrifice.

THE LAMB!

The Father knew the only way mankind could be set free for eternity was for His Son to become the final offering for sin. No more altars with the blood of birds, bulls, lambs or goats.

On the cross in Jerusalem was *"The Lamb of God, which taketh away the sin of the world"* (John 1:29).

Animal sacrifices were only a temporary

covering, a Band-Aid®, if you will. The blood of Jesus would take care of all iniquity—past, present and future.

"CRUCIFY HIM!"

It was Passover. Jerusalem was packed and bustling with people from all over the known world. Each family brought their special lamb to be offered. The priests were at the temple, busy with their sacrificial services.

> The blood of Jesus would take care of all iniquity—past, present and future.

In the court of Herod, Jesus was put on trial and —yet Pilate said, *"I find no fault in this man"* (Luke 23:4).

Pilate knew the Passover tradition of setting a prisoner free, so he presented two men to the crowd, Jesus and Barabbas, believing they would want to see Jesus liberated. Instead, the throng yelled, "Free Barabbas!" (v.18).

Once more, Pilate presented Jesus to be freed, but the people chanted, *"Crucify him, crucify him"* (v.21).

God's only Son, Jesus, was sentenced to die on the cross.

THE PROPHECY

Hundreds of years before Jesus was ever born, David wrote Psalm 22, which contains ten direct references to the day Christ was crucified:

One: *"My God, my God, why hast thou forsaken me?"* (Psalm 22:1). These are the exact words Christ spoke on the cross (Matthew 27:46; Mark 15:34).

Two: *"All they that see me laugh me to scorn ...saying, He trusted on the Lord that he would deliver him"* (vv.7-8). At Calvary, the scribes and elders mocked, *"He trusted in God; let him deliver him now"* (Matthew 27:43).

Three: *"...for there is none to help"* (Psalm 22:11). The disciples had abandoned Him.

Four: *"Many bulls have compassed me..."* (v.12). Bulls represent the demons of evil who had

Him surrounded.

Five: *"My strength is dried up like a potsherd; and my tongue cleaveth to my jaws; and thou hast brought me into the dust of death"* (v.15). On the cross, *"Jesus knowing that all things were now accomplished, that the scripture might be fulfilled, saith, I thirst"* (John 19:28).

Six: *"For dogs have compassed me: the assembly of the wicked have enclosed me: they pierced my hands and my feet"* (Psalm 22:16). The dogs symbolize the Romans who tormented Christ and there is evidence of His hands and feet being pierced (John 10:25,27).

Seven: *"I may tell all my bones: they look and stare upon me"* (Psalm 22:17). Many gathered at the foot of the cross, *"And sitting down they watched him there"* (Matthew 27:36).

Eight: David wrote, *"They part my garments among them, and cast lots upon my vesture"* (Psalm 22:18). In the Gospel according to Matthew, *"And they crucified him, and parted his garments, casting lots: that it might be fulfilled which was spoken by the prophet"* (Matthew 27:35).

Nine: *"Save me from the Lion's mouth..."* (Psalm 22:21). The lion represents the Roman government.

Ten: The psalmist declares, *"Ye that fear the Lord, praise him; all ye the seed of Jacob, glorify him; and fear him, all ye the seed of Israel"* (v.32). The Christ of Calvary, *"...was made of the seed of David according to the flesh"* (Romans 1:3).

> *The enemy planned the cross for death, but God planned it for life.*

What a prophecy! The enemy planned the cross for death, but God planned it for life.

THE FINAL WORDS

The Roman soldiers nailed Jesus on the cross and placed it at Golgotha, a prominent spot in Jerusalem. He hung between two thieves.

At three o'clock in the afternoon, the high priest would take his knife and cut the throat of the Pascal lamb—the last lamb of Passover. On this life-changing day, both the priest and Jesus called out the same words at the same time: "It is finished!"

What a difference between the two events. At the next Passover there would need to be another lamb, but Jesus became the final sacrifice for man's sin.

Suddenly, when Christ uttered those final words, *"...behold, the veil of the temple was rent in twain from the top to the bottom; and the earth did quake, and the rocks rent"* (Matthew 27:51).

The veil was cut in half by God so He could come to man and sinners would now be able enter into the Holy of Holies.

Satan thought the final chapter had been written, yet this was just the start.

Our Heavenly Father already knew the end of this story since the plan was laid from the foundations of the world.

Satan thought the final chapter had been written, yet this was just the start. Jesus would soon ascend back to the Father and place His blood on the altar (Hebrews 9:24-26).

The precious blood of Christ provided atonement so that you and I can gain full access into the very presence of God.

Because of the cross we can have eternal redemption. *"For God so loved the world, that he gave his only begotten Son, that whosoever believeth in him should not perish, but have everlasting life"* (John 3:16).

THE ULTIMATE VICTORY

On these pages you have seen how the Lord will cause the weapons of your enemies to either become their own destruction, or bring honor and glory to God:

- Goliath's was decapitated with his own sword.
- The lions were supposed to destroy Daniel, but instead they devoured his enemies.

- Haman was hung on the very gallows he built to hang Mordecai.
- The dark pit Joseph endured had a purpose which saved the Israelites from famine.
- Shadrach, Meshach and Abednego survived the fiery furnace and revival came to Babylon.
- Satan attempts to destroy lives through violence and the shedding of human blood, but the blood of Christ provides the remission for our sin.
- The devil uses his words against us, but they are powerless compared to the Word of God.
- The cross was to be Christ's final defeat, but it was only His triumphant start.

When Jesus uttered "It is finished" He meant it! The battle has already been fought and won and *"No weapon that is formed against thee shall prosper..."* (Isaiah 54:17).

Today, victory is yours!

NOTES

_____

_____

_____

_____

_____

_____

_____

_____

_____

_____

_____

_____

_____

_____

_____

FOR BOOKS AND MEDIA RESOURCES
OR TO SCHEDULE THE AUTHOR FOR SPEAKING
ENGAGEMENTS, CONTACT:

TOMMY COMBS
HEALING WORD
LIVING WORD MINISTRIES
P.O. BOX 1000
DORA, AL 35062

PHONE: 1-866-392WORD (9673)
INTERNET: www.tommycombs.org
EMAIL: tommy@tommycombs.org